Iguana as Pets

The Ultimate Pet Guide for Iguanas

General Info, Purchasing, Care, Cost, Keeping, Health, Supplies, Food, Breeding and More Included!

By Lolly Brown

Foreword

The original range of iguanas is naturally found in Central America, southern Mexico, and most of South America. Almost all throughout the day, Iguanas spend their time high in the forest canopy. They are diurnal meaning that the time they are most active is during the day and they sleep at night. Iguanas have natural green and brown colors of the scale. With the help of their color contrast, it is easier for them to hide themselves from predators. Iguanas can be territorial especially the male ones. They may display head bobbing, hissing, and tail twitching.

If you are planning to buy this kind of pet, you must make sure that you are well-informed with its biological information, temperament, and specific needs. All you need is enough time, effort, and this book to do so! You must make sure that you are capable of handling it properly and that you are physically, emotionally, and financially ready in order to become a responsible pet owner. Get ready as this book will discuss everything you need to know about iguanas; from their heritage, physique, down to their special and specific needs in terms of its health, nutrition, grooming, habitat, maintenance, and well-being.

Table of Contents

Chapter One: Biological Information

Iguanas are one of the most well-known lizards. They are docile and make great pets as they are very easy to handle and take care of. Before you decide whether or not an Iguana is the ideal pet for you, you must be able to know the basic information like its heritage, behavior, and sub-species. Dealing with Iguanas is going to be a long term commitment therefore you must really make sure that you are ready in all aspects. In this chapter you will receive an introduction to the iguana breed which includes its general information and biological facts. A list of its sub – species will also be given.

Taxonomy, Origin and Distribution

Iguanas have a scientific name of *Iguana Iguana*. They belong in Kingdom *Animalia*, Phylum *Chordata*, Class *Reptilia*, Order *Squamata*, Suborder *Sauria* Family *Iguanidae* Genus *Iguana*, and Species *Iguana*

The original range of iguanas is naturally found in Central America, southern Mexico, and most of South America. A small population of it can also be found on the Lesser Antilles islands. In a few parts of Florida, Hawaii, and California is where the wild iguanas are settling. Either the escaped from captivity or they have been intentionally released by their past owners.

Though they seem balancing the ecosystem of their new habitat, they are becoming harmful to native species as they are preying on their resources. It has been actually forbidden in Hawaii to take care of Iguanas for this matter. Owning an Iguana entails full responsibility and conscious effort in order to prevent them from entering the wild on which they are considered non-native species.

They are considered as arboreal which means that they live in trees. Their long claws are very essential in order to keep up with this lifestyle. They may seem clumsy as they keep on knocking things, falling of perches, or even tipping over furniture, still they can be considered as good climbers. Almost all throughout the day, Iguanas spend their time high in the forest canopy. They only try to reach the ground if they want to move from tree to tree, if they need to mate, or lay eggs. They are good jumpers and swimmers as well.

They are diurnal meaning that the time they are most active is during the day and they sleep at night. They are fully awake the whole day and sleep through the whole night. Feral Iguanas or Iguanas living in the wild usually wake up when the sun comes up and they will move to a location on which they can warm themselves up to get going and they will start to find food during mid-late morning.

Size, Life Span, and Physical Appearance

Iguanas have natural green and brown colors of the scale. With the help of their color contrast, it is easier for them to hide themselves from predators. They can blend well with the surrounding forest and they will keep still until their predator is gone. They weigh around 4 to 8 kilos and can grow to over 2 meter in length. With proper husbandry, they are expected to live 15 to 20 years of age.

Sub – Species of Iguanas

Iguanas have six main sub species. Read carefully and find out which type of Iguana will best suit you and your family as well.

Genus Cyclura - Rock Iguanas

Distribution: West India

Physical characteristics:

Length: 5 feet

Body: Its body color varies. They can be gray, green, blue, brown or even bright red.

Behavior and Nature: Males are considered gregarious at a young age but they get to be more aggressive as they grow old. They are territorial as they compete for females. Females, on the other hand, are more tolerant of each other except the time on which they have just laid their eggs

Genus Amblyrhyncus - Marine Iguana

Distribution: Rocky waters and mangroves found in Galapagos Islands

Physical characteristics:

Length: 3 to 5 feet

Body: They exhibit a reddish coloration that resembles a mixture of jagged rocks and coral reef.

Behavior and Nature: They have the ability to forage under water.

Genus Conolophus - Land Iguanas

Distribution: Galapagos Islands

Physical characteristics:

Length: 3 to 5 feet

Body: Their colors range between brown, yellow, red, and dark gray

Behavior and Nature: They tend to display territorial behaviors especially the males.

Genus Ctenosauria - Spiny Tailed Iguanas

Distribution: Mexico and Central America

Physical characteristics:

Length: 5 inches to 4 feet

Body: They have spiny scales found in their back and tail. Their colors range from orange, green, brown, bright yellow, and gray.

Behavior and Nature: Territorial displays such as body inflation, rapid nodding, and color changes are shown by the males whenever there is a need to defend their colony

Genus Dipsosaurus- Desert Iguanas

Distribution: Mexico and Southwestern United States

Physical characteristics:

Length: 16 inches

Body: They have the capacity to change color from gray to white

Behavior and Nature: They can move around even under extreme heat. They are considered as good climbers

Genus Sauromalus- Chuckwalla

Distribution: Northern Mexico ad Southwestern United States

Physical characteristics:-

Length: 15 to 30 inches

Body: Males are usually covered in red or orange color while the females have yellowish spots or gray found on their backs

Behavior and Nature: They are very territorial in nature especially the males. Whenever they feel that they are in danger they will find a crevice and hide.

Quick Facts

Distribution and Range: Central America, Southern Mexico, and South America

Breed Size: small to medium sized breed

Body Type and Appearance: They display a stocky stature; they have saggy skin found on their throats; their spine runs along their head, neck, back, and tail.

Length: 3 to 6 feet

Weight: Weighs an average of 4 to 8 kilos

Skin Texture: scaly texture

Color: Their colors depend on the specie they belong. In general they have green, yellow, and brown color.

Temperament: They are docile and easy to take care of; they can also be territorial especially the males

Diet: They feed on different kinds of insects, fruits and leaves

Habitat: Lowland tropical forest on which they have access to water to deserted places depending on which specie they belong

Health Conditions: Generally healthy but predisposed to common illnesses such as egg binding, metabolic bone disease, burns, dehydration, shedding, and respiratory infections

Lifespan: They can live an average life of 15 to 20 years

Chapter Two: Iguanas as Pets

After gaining knowledge on all the basic information about iguanas, we hope that you're now gaining insight about this exotic pet but it doesn't stop there. It is only just the beginning! Before you make a decision if an iguana is the ideal pet for you, there are still many things for you to discover. With the aid of this chapter, you will be able to delve more vital information you need to know in order to make sure that this pet is the right kind for you and your family. We'll discuss its behavior, legal requirements in order to keep one, as well as an overview of the cost it entails.

Behavioral Characteristics and Interaction

Just like human beings, an iguana is uniquely different from other species of its own kind. Some iguanas may act a little scared or aggressive but in general, they are a calm type. As long as they stay happy and feel safe, they will be able to develop more positive traits and become a rewarding exotic pet.

If you purchased a juvenile iguana, as it grows old, it will develop through stages of changes and will go in the direction of its inherent or natural characteristics. Some may have temperamental changes that are only temporary and can be reversed back to normal. The season and other environmental factors can trigger the change in behavior of iguanas.

Having a pet is like a gamble, you'll be wishing that it'll turn out to be a great pet without a hundred percent assurance. But if you are knowledgeable enough, you'll be able to shape or hone the characteristics of your pet and make it as pleasant as possible. The way you raise your iguana is where there hope of becoming properly tamed relies on.

Expect that during the first days, the iguana will look afraid as there is a tendency that it will feel intimidated by its owner's size. Do not get frustrated if this happens since it is just natural. Wait until your pet has fully adjusted. Have yourself familiarized by visiting your pet's enclosure every day. If properly socialized, they can get along well with other animals as well as other people besides its owner.

Iguanas can be territorial especially the male ones. They may display head bobbing, hissing, and tail twitching as signs that they are being defensive. They may try to compress their body laterally in order for to look taller and intimidating.

Iguanas to other Pets

Iguanas, if socialized properly, can be introduced to a variety of other pets. If you're going to introduce a smaller pet like bird, beware of potential aggression that your iguana might display as they are really against "small intruders." Each introduction will be different as pet varies from each other. Sometimes it goes smoothly and sometimes not. Make sure that you are supervising your pet when your iguana socializes with others to prevent any trouble. Always allow escape routes so that if ever one of them feels the need to retreat from the other, it can easily go.

Keeping an Iguana

Before anything else, you must first know the specie you are interested in. You should gather all the information you need in order to be well educated with regard to the pet you want to have. You should be able to answer generic questions like how much will it cost, how big will it get, what kind of food does it eat, what kind of care does it require, etc. So that if ever your family ask about these questions, you'll be knowledgeable enough to answer it with confidence. Giving them the right answers can help them see how eager and willing you are to own an iguana.

Everything takes time and you shouldn't rush things. Do not immediately drop the news that you want an iguana as a pet especially if the members of your family are uptight with this idea. Instead, you can give them hints that you are being fond of snakes lately. You can tell them stories about the iguana owners you know and their experiences in taking care of an iguana. By this way, they'll know that it isn't really that hard to maintain an iguana and they might even be an ideal pet for the family.

It is very unlikely that your family members or roommates will accept the idea overnight. If ever they still stand against it do not be angry or feel frustrated. It might take weeks, months, or even years. Just be patient encouraging them in the best possible way you can. Just be calm and do your best in persuading them. You'll surely win their favor when you talk it to them constantly.

No matter how much you like having an iguana as your pet you must still consider your housemates' decision. If they do not really approve, wait until they do so. You must respect their feelings towards it as it is not only you who's going to deal with the snake but they will too. In that case, it is better for you not to buy at all. If you disregard their opinion about it, it may just cause you a problem. It might be the root of misunderstanding. You may be forced to re-locate your pet or bring it shelters and have it for adoption.

If ever your roommate or family saw how willing and able you are to take care of an iguana, this can be a great factor in order to make them say yes with it. Show them that you will be able to commit yourself with your potential pet and that you will be responsible enough to provide it with their needs.

Pros and Cons of Iguana

Pros

- Its food is easy to find as an iguana has a herbivore diet which means they feed on plants, vegetables, and fruits alone.
- This specie can get along well with other animals.
- They are easy to accommodate as their rate of activity is mild and they sleep at night.
- Losing a pet is one of the hardest aspects of owning a pet; luckily iguanas can live up to the extent of 20 years.
- They can be affectionate if properly tamed.

Cons

- Iguanas can be quite aggressive.
- Taking an exotic animal to the vet will cost you more than taking a dog or a cat to the vet.
- They require lots of space.
- They eat a lot so you have to restock more often.
- They require much time and attention.
- Not as receptive as other animals like cats and dogs.
- Can be easily trained, tamed, and socialize.
- May not be a typical pet that everyone in the household is fond of.

- Can live up to 20 years or more which means that long – term commitment is needed.

Do You Need a License or Permit?

CITES or the Convention on International Trade in Endangered Species for wild fauna and flora is the one responsible for taking care of plants and animals of different species especially the ones who are considered as endangered. This organization is vocal to their advocacy against over-exploitation of animals and plants through international trade. Roughly 30,000 species of plants and 5,800 species of animals are being protected by CITES.

Convention on International Trade in Endangered Species for wild fauna and flora has 3 appendices. In each appendix is a list of different plant and animal species categorized differently with regard to its rules in exporting, keeping, and trading. Appendix I is composed of species that are considered as most endangered among any other animals and plants listed by CITES. These species are threatened with extinction. Appendix II is a list of species that are not necessarily threatened with extinction now but the probability of it depends on how closely controlled the trade is. This is where iguana belongs. Appendix III is full of species requested by different parties that regulate trade in the species resulting to the need of cooperation from other countries in order to prevent illegal or unsustainable exploitation.

In general, you don't need to have approval from wildlife organizations or authorities in order to have your iguana licensed. All you have to do is to provide a document with the name, identity of the specie on which your pet belongs. There is a need for you to give information like name, address, contact details, and the signature of the previous owner or on where you bought your pet is also needed. You also have to provide your personal information and contact information. This kind of document needs to be kept for future reference for you as the new owner of the iguana until it is sold or if it dies.

Cost of Owning an Iguana

Having pets, in general, can be expensive regardless if it's a low maintenance or a high maintenance one. Either of the two, you need to provide them enough supplies essential for them to keep up with a healthy lifestyle. Though iguanas seems like small creatures that are easy to handle and to maintain, the truth is they doesn't come cheap at all! It is necessary for you to provide everything that your pet needs in order for it to live happy and satisfied.

The cost will vary depending on where you have purchased the supplies, the nutrient content of the food you are going to provide, the size and quality of the enclosure, the time being, the kind of equipment your iguana needs, etc. All these expenses might be quite overwhelming and so you must really prepare yourself and your wallet as well for you to be able to attend all the costs it entails.

Through this section, you'll be given an overview of the expenses you might have to manage in order to keep and purchase a snake, as well as the supplies needed for maintenance, food, enclosures or its habitat, veterinary care, and other on-going essential costs that you have to cover. The cost of the iguana itself, accessories, substrate, initial medical check-ups, licensing, equipment, and food are just some of the expenses you have to initially cover.

Purchase price of iguana: $30 to $100 above

The costs of iguanas depend on its size, age, specie, and the place where you bought it. You may expect the amount of $30 to $100 and more for an iguana being sold by a reputable breeder, in general. It is better for you to spend a huge amount of money in the start given that you are sure that the iguana is well-raised as for the reason that it came from a highly-regarded breeder rather than buy a cheaper one from an irresponsible breeder as it may be suffering from behavioral problems and infections that may lead to a bigger expense in the future.It is highly recommended for you to buy only from reputable and legit breeders to ensure that the iguana you are going to purchase is healthy and as a much as possible is a captive-bred. You may buy from online stores or websites as well as on reptile conventions. Ask for referrals to ensure that you will be able to deal with a well-regarded breeder alone.

Enclosure: $90 or more

Iguanas can grow as large as 6 feet when they reach adulthood. You must ensure that the enclosure you'll be purchasing is large enough for all the habitat necessities with a remaining free space for your pet to roam around. The enclosure of your pet should be at least twice its length and should be tall. Purchase or build is either made out of thick plywood or thick glass/ plexiglass.

Substrate: $10 to $20

Make sure that you'll be able to provide the best kind of substrate for your pet. You can use paper towels, alfalfa pellets, and wrapping paper. Avoid using bark, rocks, gravel, cob, con, cat litter, potting soil, or wood shavings.

Cage Accessories: $10 to $25

In order to simulate a healthy environment for your pet, you should be able to set up its terrarium as if it's living in the wild. You may add cage decors such as branches, leaves, live plants, and other things that would make the cage pleasing to the eyes. It is up to you what supplies or accessories to use. Just make sure that you will not overdo it. Just make sure there will be enough space for your pet to walk around.

Food: $15 above

Iguanas feed on plants, vegetables, and fruits. You can feed your pet with greens including turnip, collard, romaine lettuce, and kale.

Veterinary Care: $75 to $100 or more

It is advisable for your pet to visit the vet once in a while for a routine check-up in order to make sure that its health is exceptional. Just like humans, iguanas can also get sick. You should also save a budget for medical or lab tests just in case your pet will need such procedures. You may spend $75 to $100.

Lighting and Heating Equipment: $100 or more

Iguanas are in need of UV radiation specifically UVA and UVB. The use of an artificial UV bulb is highly advisable especially if you live in a place where your pet cannot bask under the sun daily.

Chapter Three: How to Acquire Iguanas

After getting to know your potential pet, it's now time for you to learn how to spot a healthy breed and how to find a reputable and trustworthy breeder to deal with. You must really pay attention to all the factors you have to consider and one of it is the place and to whom you can acquire a healthy Iguana breed. The way the Iguana has been raised is a vital part on the attitude and behavior of it. Therefore you should really be meticulous on choosing a reputable breeder.

In this chapter you will be provided with places you can buy your pet, the criteria on selecting a healthy Iguana and be given criteria to spot a reputable and trustworthy breeder.

Where to Purchase an Iguana

There are lots of places to choose from with regard to buying an Iguana. The place where you can find and purchase a good Iguana breed can be quite confusing but you should always look after a reputable place as the environment where it has been raised or where it stayed can greatly affect its attitude and behavior.

Private breeders

You have to take precautions when you are going to deal with private breeders. You can ask the right questions so that you'll be able to check whether the breeder is trustworthy or not.

Pros

- Private breeders are the ones taking care of the iguanas personally therefore you'll be able to see if they are reputable or not depending on how the iguanas are being raised
- They don't only take care of iguanas for profit but they do it for the sake of their care for this specie
- Usually, pets being bred by private breeders are well-taken care of.

Cons

- You have to visit personally the location of the private breeder which can be inconvenient if your place is far from it.
- There is a need for you to personally pick up the pet which can cost you transportation expenses

Reptile Shop

It is highly recommended among expert and novice iguana keepers including reptile enthusiasts and veterinarians.

Pros

- In reptile shops, you can ask questions about the pet you are about to purchase
- Usually, the staff are accommodating and have wide knowledge about the species they sell
- You may find a variety of iguanas here compared to other commercial pet stores. It means that you'll have more options to choose from

Cons

- Some animal groups consider any kind of pet shops as a "bad industry" since they claim that pet stores aren't taking care of pets as their own but they keep them for the mere purpose of profit. As they have sold and emptied one cage they will immediately restock it.

Reptile shows

These conventions are usually crowded with reptile's enthusiasts, check out the pros and cons below:

Pros

- You can buy a healthy iguana with a cheaper price. This is ideal especially if your budget is limited
- You can meet different reptile owners and enthusiasts
- There's a bigger possibility that the breeders here are trustworthy as they have been invited in the event

Cons

- This is not an annual event. There is a chance that you'll have to wait for months for the next event as these aren't a daily thing which can be a problem if you want to have an iguana right at the moment.

Local Rescue Center

This is where you can adopt iguanas that have been abandoned by their previous owners or have been found roaming around the city/area.

Pros

- You can have a fully grown iguana without the need of enduring its growing years
- You can give a new home to those that have been abandoned by their past owners
- It's like saving a life and bringing hope to animals

Cons

- The availability of iguanas itself vary
- There may not be enough options you may choose from as the kinds of species here are limited

How to Spot a Reputable Iguana Breeder

Finding a highly regarded breeder is essential as it mirrors the characteristics instilled upon the animals he raise. If the breeder is caring and responsible, then there's a big chance that the iguanas he breed are raised in a good and healthy environment.

Characteristics of a Reputable Iguana Breeder

- He must be knowledgeable about iguanas and must be able to give information that is not common. If they only supply you with general information that even a pet store clerk can give, it means that he is not that interested with the pet he is selling.

- The reason why he is breeding iguanas should be because of its health or because it is his hobby and not primarily for the reason of profit.

- He should be able to give you some points on how to take care of it and give you directions on how to set up its enclosure as well as the specific needs of iguanas

- He should be friendly as a reputable breeder builds a good relationship with his existing and potential buyers.

- He should ask you questions about yourself as a legit breeder wants to know if he is also dealing with a person who's willing and able to take care of an iguana.

- He should be patient. He should not get irritated if you asked him many questions. He should enthusiastically answer all the inquiries you've got and he should even share facts without the need of asking

Tips in Finding a Reputable Iguana Breeder

- Ask for referrals. Inquire in veterinary offices, iguana owners, and pet stores.

- Check the website of the breeder if there's any. His license and full contact details should be given. If the website looks suspicious, do not waste your time and just find another breeder.

- You may call the breeder and conduct a small interview over the phone. Ask for his history and experience in taking care of an iguana.

- Try to ask if you can visit his facilities and if the breeder agrees there's a big chance that you are dealing with a reputable one.

Characteristics of a Healthy Breed

Eyes

Make sure that eyes of the iguana are clear and free from any discharge. If ever the iguana's eyes have signs of cloudiness, find another one as it may indicate illness.

Breathing

Observe how the iguana breathes. There should be no sign of labour breathing. Check its nostrils. Make sure it's free from any discharge as well.

Body

The iguana's body should be free from any blisters, parasites, injury, and body abnormalities. It should be able to move freely and should not have any mobility issues. When you lift it up, you should be able to feel a sense of strength to its body.

Behavior

The iguana should be active and alert to its environment at all times. It should not display lethargy as it is one sign of having a sickness.

Important Reminder:

It is highly advisable for you to choose an iguana that is bred in captivity as feral or wild iguana can potentially carry health problems. Captive bred iguanas are easier to handle and socialized with people.

List of Breeders and Rescue Websites

To help you narrow down your choices, here is a list of breeders and adoption rescue websites around the United States and the United Kingdom you may opt to look into:

United States Breeders and Rescue Websites

Florida Iguana & Tortoise Breeders

<https://www.floridaiguana.com/>

US Iguana

<http://www.boalab.com/>

Underground Reptiles

<https://undergroundreptiles.com/product-category/animals/lizards/iguanas/>

Snakes at Sunset

<http://snakesatsunset.com/iguanas-for-sale/>

Kingsnake.com

<http://snakesatsunset.com/iguanas-for-sale/>

Hoobly Classifieds
<http://www.hoobly.com/184/2160/0/>

Backwater Reptiles
<http://www.backwaterreptiles.com/iguanas/green-iguana-for-sale.html/>

Reptile Rescue Orange County
<http://www.reptilerescueoc.org/>

Arrowhead Reptile Rescue
<http://www.arrowheadreptilerescue.org/adopt/>

Beautiful Dragons Reptile Rescue
<http://www.beautifuldragons.com/rescue.html>

Texas Reptile and Small Animal Rescue
<http://www.texasreptilerescue.com/>

United Kingdom Breeders and Rescue Websites

Pets4Homes

<https://www.pets4homes.co.uk/pet-advice/types-of-iguana.html?fb_comment_id=558701117511989_881661018549329#f185904256a8ffc/>

Gumtree

<https://www.gumtree.com/reptiles/uk/iguana/>

Preloved UK

<http://www.preloved.co.uk/classifieds/pets/reptiles/for-sale/uk/green+iguanas/>

Exotic Pets

<https://www.exotic-pets.co.uk/green-iguana.html/>

RSPA Reptile Rescue

<http://www.rspcareptilerescue.co.uk/>

Reptile Rescue Centre

<https://www.hd-reptiles.co.uk/g-d-reptiles-rescue-and-re-homing-centre/>

Chapter Four: Habitat Needs of Your Iguanas

After learning how to spot a healthy breed as well as a well-regarded breeder, it's now to for you to gain knowledge on how you'll be able to provide a healthy habitat for your iguana. The environment your iguana lives in is a great factor you must consider as it can affect the mood and behavior of your pet. It is vital for you to provide them with the best place to dwell in order to keep your pet happy and satisfied with the new environment it belongs.

This chapter we'll help you know more about its environmental needs like how to house them, the materials you need to use, and other housing points you'll need to know to make sure that your pet will be happy and satisfied with living in its new home.

Cage Considerations for Iguanas

Cage Size

When buying a cage, the first thing you have to consider is the size of it. You should realize that iguanas can grow as long as 6 feet when they reach adulthood. You must ensure that the enclosure you'll be purchasing is large enough for all the habitat necessities with a free space for your pet to roam around.

The enclosure of your pet should be at least twice its length and should be tall. Remember that iguanas are arboreal which means they are fond of living and climbing trees and that they feel most comfortable when they are located at a high place. Six feet is the minimum required size of the cage. The width, on the other hand, should be at least half its length. Although a juvenile or baby iguana does not need a large enclosure, take note that this specie grow throughout its lifetime. Therefore, it is important for you to plan ahead and buy a large cage already so that your pet will not outgrow its enclosure.

Cage Material

Make sure that the enclosure you will purchase or build is either made out of thick plywood or thick glass/ Plexiglass because iguanas have very sharp claws that can easily rip or damage the enclosure if it's made out of mesh or low quality materials.

Cage Safety

You should know that iguanas are fond of escaping. They will try to find a way out. In that case, make sure that the enclosure you'll be providing for your pet has lids and safety latches on it to prevent them from going out of their cage.

Substrate

Choosing the right substrate is essential in maintaining the comfort as well as the humidity inside the cage. Provide a thick layer of substrate for your pet's enclosure. You can use paper towels, alfalfa pellets, and wrapping paper. Avoid using bark, rocks, gravel, cob, con, cat litter, potting soil, or wood shavings. These materials are unsafe for your pet as they have the tendency to ingest it and may cause impactions or damage in the intestine.

Spag Moss/Plants

For a large enclosure, you may use two to three bags of it. This is essential for absorbing moisture to prevent molds from accumulating inside the enclosure. You may mix spag moss with the bedding of the enclosure. This will add texture to the enclosure as well. If you are planning to add plants for aesthetic or humidity purposes, make sure it is placed properly on which your pet will not be able to break or damage it. Iguanas grow very large and there's a tendency that they will break something inside the cage like accessories inside the enclosure.

Water bowls

Make sure that the size of the water bowl is appropriate for the size of your pet. Your iguana should have an access to fresh drinking water at all times. Ensure that the water bowl cannot be tipped over by your pet. Usually, iguanas tend to immerse themselves in water and so it is ideal for you to provide them with a larger container. Always check on the amount of water left in the bowl. Replace and replenish the water regularly.

Temperature and Lighting

Iguana's need their enclosure to be kept very warm. The ambient air surrounding the enclosure should not be lower than 80 degrees Fahrenheit. It is very essential for you to maintain and regulate the correct temperature for your pet. The enclosure should also be properly lit

Types of Lighting/Heating Equipment

UV Light

Iguanas are in need of UV radiation specifically UVA and UVB. UVA is necessary for their sense of well-being and for them to feel good. UVB, on the other hand, is needed to properly synthesize Vitamin D which is essential for absorbing calcium from the food that they are about to digest. It is vital for keeping the bones strong. The use of an artificial UV bulb is highly advisable especially if you live in a place where your pet cannot bask under the sun daily.

- **Fluorescent Tubes** - This is the most accessible type of UV lamp or bulb. Just like how natural sunlight is, it needs to be set up properly in order to mimic a natural light. Make sure that you'll acquire a bulb that's especially made for reptiles since ordinary full-spectrum fluorescent bulbs do not produce enough amount of UVB. You may install multiple tubes inside the enclosure to emit proper levels of UVB. It is best to replace the fluorescent tubes every six to nine months since by this time the amount of UV degrades.

- **Mercury Vapor Lamps** - This looks like incandescent bulbs. It is a new way to provide UVB for your pet. Using Mega-Ray MV bulb by Westron lighting/ Mac Industries is highly recommended by Green Iguana Society as it gives off an exceptional level of UVB and has a lower decay rate compared to other brands.

Humidity

Iguanas need high humidity inside their enclosure. The proper level of humidity they require is between 65% and 75%. One way of increasing humidity is through spritzing the cage as well as your pet with water several times a day or you can place a humidifier in the room where your iguana's enclosure is located and even an ultrasonic fogger inside its enclosure.

Chapter Five: The Right Diet for Your Iguana

A very common myth about iguanas is that these creatures are carnivores, what most people especially first time keepers don't know is that iguanas are strict herbivores! Needless to say, these pets are vegetarian. They only eat plant or flower based matter, and if you stick in giving them an all plant diet, it'll ensure that their skin or scale colors will remain vibrant including green, oranges, red, and blue type of iguanas. If you feed your iguana with any type of meat or animal protein like insects, it will surely shorten their lives, suffer from illnesses, and make their skin color turn dull over time. It could also cause them to develop aggressive behaviors.

The Right Herbivore Diet

Not all vegetables and fruits are healthy for iguanas! A major example is a head lettuce, feeding your iguana with such veggie is like feeding them with paper because it has no nutritional value for them. Some plants and flowers could also be toxic as well as acidic fruits including oranges, grapefruits, lemons, limes, kiwis, and pineapples shouldn't be fed to iguanas as much as possible. In general their diet consists of fibrous plants. Iguanas don't eat much fruit in the wild but since it's in captivity, it's also recommended that you feed it with a healthy amount of fruits once in a while.

There's a lot of conflicting information about the "proper" or standard iguana diet but one thing that should be consistent is that you have to make sure that there's a calcium and phosphorus ratio of 2:1. You can check out further information on the nutrient ratio of each veggies/fruits in the Green Iguana Society website or other forum sites as well. You can also ask your vet about the recommended food ratios for your iguana. In addition, if you want to give your iguana a calcium supplement just sprinkle it on top of its food.

Recommended Vegetable and Fruit Diet

Vegetables should make up 40 - 45% of your iguana's diet while fruits should make up 10% or less, and should be fed no more than twice a week.

Here is the list of veggies and fruits for your iguana:

Staple Veggies/Flowers

- Turnip Greens and Veggies
- Curly Mustart/Mustart
- Marigold (occasional)
- Red and Green Basil
- Peppermint
- Spearmint
- Alfalfa Plant
- Nasturtium Leaves and Flower
- Coriander/ Cilantro
- Dahlia (occas)
- Collard Greens
- Rocket
- Thyme
- Hibiscus (leaves/flowers)
- Rosemary
- Dandelion greens

- Watercress
- Butternut squash
- Green beans
- Okra
- Parsnips
- Snap peas
- Bellpeppers (great color enhancer)
- Escarole
- Arugala
- Acorn Squash

Staple Fruits

- Cactus Leaves
- Mango
- Papaya
- Banana
- Melon
- Blackberries/Raspberries (occasional)

Toxic Foods

Animals to avoid:

Insects, worms, mice, pinky mice

All dairy products:

Milk, Cheese, Yogurt, Eggs

Pet Foods

Dog food, Cat food, Canned foods, Bird feeds, etc.

Meat or Animal

Beef, Chicken, Pork, Turkey

Rhubarb (poisonous and deadly to iguana species)

<u>**Important Reminder:**</u>

The rule of thumb when you're feeding your iguana a veggie diet is: the more varied the better. Of course, you won't be able to find all of the recommended veggies and fruits listed above in in one place, so it's up to you to explore where you can find other types of veggie around your area that can't always be found in the grocery store. You would want to have a nice variety of food but not too much.

Preparing Your Iguana Food

You need to cut the veggies in bite – size pieces, other pet owners like to grate it or chop it finely. Now of course, the size of those pieces should depend on how large or small your iguana is, so just adjust accordingly. It goes the same for fruits. When it comes to fruits though, you might need to peel off the skin especially if you think it doesn't look good for consumption, it's also best to seed the fruits; there are also some fruits wherein you can leave the skin, it depends on you if you want to feed it to your iguana.

After washing the fruits and vegetables with water (make sure that the bowls you're using are also thoroughly washed so as to avoid chemical left over from soaps/detergents since these can be toxic for your iguana), you can then feed it to your pet or what you can do is soak it in water then drain it out before placing it in a tightly secured tupperware so that it'll stay fresh. Every morning when you take it out, you can just rinse it again in the water

Tip:

If you bought a lot of veggies that's about good for a week or so, you can place the excess veggies in a zip lock bag and place it in the freezer, then just pop it in the microwave to heat it up a bit (about 2 minutes tops) whenever you're going to feed your pet again. Just a word of caution, if the veggies or fruit is too hot, doesn't feed it to your iguana directly, let it cool down.

Food Serving Tips

- You should only feed your iguana as he's going to finish in one serving.

- Don't feed your iguana with only one type of veggie for every serving. You need to mix two or three veggies together otherwise your pet can become quite picky.

- Yellow - colored veggies like squash can be fed to your pet daily.

- You can purchase mixed veggies from the grocery store but just feed it to your pet at least once a week and not every day. Before feeding peas or mixed veggies to your iguana make sure that you soak it first with water to make it soft and easily digestible.

- Just like any other animals, you need to provide fresh and clean water for your pet. If you don't see it drinking enough water, what you can do to encourage it is that you can place a small piece of food near its water bowl so that it'll remember to drink. And then each day, what you can do is to reduce the size of the treat just so your pet can form a habit of drinking water every day.

Frequency and Amount of Feeding

Feeding your pet iguana should be done daily. You can feed it either 2 to 3 times a day. Just make sure you feed them daily so that they'll stay healthy.

When it comes to the amount, as I've mentioned earlier, it highly depends on the age, the size and even the appetite of the iguana. You won't have to worry about overfeeding your pet because they'll only eat what they want to eat. You'll soon know how much to feed your pet or the kinds of food that your iguana prefers once you spend enough time with it, which is why it's highly recommended that you keep track of its eating habits, take notes of the daily serving you're giving, and observe what makes your pet want to eat more or the time of day it prefers.

If ever your iguana has left overs it's best to remove it so as not to risk eating rotten food and maintain the cage's cleanliness. This is why it's best to not give too much, just feed what you think is enough, and just add some more if need be.

Hand – feeding Your Iguana

Hand - feeding your iguana is an ideal thing to do especially while the creature is still young or a baby iguana so that it'll get use to your smell and lessen the development of aggression such as biting. It'll be much easier to tame it in the future if you start hand – feeding it at a young age as well. However, it's also important to note that you don't also hand feed your pet everyday otherwise it may not eat any other way. Just do it from time to time but of course, be very wary and practice caution especially once they become large creatures. Always pay attention whenever you're hand – feeding them so that you'll be safe from any injuries.

Chapter Six: Body Language of Iguanas

Common pets like dogs, birds, and cats usually have their own communication style; they bark, chirp or just sit on their owner's lap. When it comes to reptiles, their behaviors and the way they send a message to their owners or to other creatures will obviously be different, which is why learning it and noticing their subtle body languages could be a great advantage so that you'll know if there is something wrong with your pet or if they simply want to show you some love.

This chapter will explain the possible meaning or indications of your pet iguana's body language. Make sure to read it because it can be very helpful for you as the owner in creating a happy relationship with your exotic pet.

To Bite or Not to Bite?

Here's the truth, keeping a wild creature like an iguana means that you'll always be at risk of being bitten. Even seasoned keepers are experiencing it from time to time. You can't help it, these are still animals at the end of the day, so make sure that before you truly decide to own one, you know what you sign up for and you're not afraid of being bitten – because you surely will!

Being bitten every now and then is part of pet keeping so better get used to it but of course still exercise caution to avoid further injuries or accidents.

Indications of Body Languages

Below are the most common body languages that your iguana may project, before you try to interpret the possible meaning of each, it's important to note that you should also see the bigger picture before assuming what they are really trying to communicate at the moment:

Dewlap Display

The dewlap is the iguana's flap on both sides of its head or neck area. This is the most obvious body language that people can notice; this is how an iguana usually communicates.

If you see their dewlaps being extended it's either, they're greeting you or trying to impress their potential mate. It's also a sign of territoriality.

An extended dewlap can also mean that the iguana is feeling threatened making it a sign of protection especially if larger creatures are around it. They use it to intimidate their potential predators in order to make themselves look bigger.

Sometimes it could just mean that they're adjusting to the temperature; they are either using it to get warmer or just trying to cool off.

Bobbing of Head

Head bobbing is another common body language for iguanas. This is more of a territorial indication. It's simply telling a message to other animals that they are in charge of the area and no other animal species should dare steal it from them. You'll notice that males usually bob their heads more than female species especially when they become mature.

If you come inside its shelter for example, it'll bob its head slowly to let you know of their presence and also recognize your presence.

If the species are bobbing rapidly, it can mean that they are feeling aggressive or agitated especially the males, so better exercise caution and don't approach them as much as possible if ever they're feeling an extreme form of irritation.

Flicking of Tongue

Usually, flicking of tongue among reptiles is a sign that they're trying to get more information about a certain environment or occurrence. They use it to make sense of their surroundings, to check out its water or food before eating it, to sense people, and other strange object as well. The only difference is that their flicking of tongue is not as developed compared to snakes and other reptiles but that is because they have better eyesight than most species.

If you see your pet doing this, it also means that it's not going to bite or at least not thinking about biting you. It usually occurs if you transfer it to a new home or if it's simply out exploring. Make sure that your house or shelter is also safe from any harm.

Sneezing

This is not really indicating any sort of behavior or it's not a form of your pet trying to send you a message, it's simply trying to get rid of their body salt. It's not also a sign of lung infection but you may need to adjust its diet if you notice the sneezes going too far or worse.

Tail Whip

Tail whip is another common form of body language among iguanas. It usually means that it's being threatened or showing some form of aggression because that's what they usually use as first defense or as a weapon against potential threats. Iguanas are actually good at whipping its tail so be very careful if you're approaching them. You'll surely see other signs like them extending of dewlap or twitching its tails before whipping its tail at you (potentially). If ever your iguana whip its tail on you, don't worry because it won't hurt that much, but just be careful so as not be whipped in the eyes.

Squirming

If your pet is squirming, it most likely means that it's not comfortable with being handled. It's either you're holding it the wrong way or it just don't feel comfortable being held at the moment.

Hatchet Mode

Usually most iguanas will stand upright whenever it is feeling "good." You might see it standing up with eyes close if you're petting it or if they're basking. So it's a sign of happiness. Now if it's in what experts called "hatchet mode," it means that they are either intimidated or aggressive, you'll see if its standing up, while it is wagging its tail or even have an extended dewlap. It can be very dangerous if such body signs combined so be very careful because it can attack you or another creature.

Digging Up

Female species usually are the ones exhibiting this kind of body language. If you see your pet digging up, it's usually a sign she is pregnant or would lay eggs in the near future. Now, if you see your pet constantly digging up for no reason (meaning they are male species or they simply just want to dig everywhere) it's a sign that your pet is not happy with his/her habitat. You might want to set it up in a better way where your pet could feel adequate.

Chapter Seven: Grooming and Maintenance Guidelines

Maintaining cleanliness in your pet's habitat is very important in providing a sanitary environment for your iguana. Keeping your pet's habitat clean is also anchored on the family or person taking care of it. If you and your pet both have good hygiene and you see to it that you're always spot cleaning its cage, you can be sure that diseases won't be spread and will not affect your pet's health as well as your family's health. In this chapter, you'll learn how to keep your pet's hygiene at par and also properly clean its habitat.

Common Questions for Maintenance and Grooming of Iguanas

Do I really need to always clean the cage/enclosure?

Yes of course! Regular cleaning prevents the possible transmission of diseases which can be found in the fecal matter of reptiles, and which may be transmissible to humans. Not only will this keep the interior of the enclosure clean, odor-free, and healthy, but it will also keep you and your family safe and healthy.

Regular cleaning is very important because it means that you thoroughly clean not just the cage of your iguana but also all the materials you placed inside the cage. Spot cleaning the interior of the cage should be done as often as possible at once every other day. When you spot clean your pet's enclosure, you should make sure that any fecal matter is removed, the shedded skin is removed as well as the uneaten or left over food. The water bowls should also be replaced more than once a week to prevent bacterial growth.

Does humidity affect the cage's cleanliness?

The humidity within the enclosure can be a perfect breeding ground for the growth of bacteria. Iguanas can be prone to skin and bacterial infection if left alone in unclean surroundings for long which is why regular cage maintenance and cleaning should be part of your routine.

What is a second terrarium/enclosure for?

Before doing a full cleanse of your pet's tank, you must first find a suitable temporary cage for your pet iguana. Check the components you need to clean and replace such as the bedding of the cage. During the cleaning process, you will need to relocate the iguana so that you can clean and sterilize the entire tank components such as its hiding spots, substrate, plants/branches etc. Make sure that it's also sufficiently ventilated.

Is it true that I always have to wash my hands before handling my pet?

Yes, actually it should be before and after. Make sure to wash your hands thoroughly, and use antibacterial soap. Properly washing your hands is not just beneficial for your pet but also for you. Spread of salmonella is very common among reptiles so make it a good habit of washing your hands.

Do I need to soak my iguana?

Yes it's a necessity but it is not because they are dirty creatures, as it's a common misconception among iguanas, they are in fact very clean animals. Usually it is their habitat that is unclean making them dirty. Soaking can also help in their shedding process as well as brush off any food stains or feces. If ever your pet defecates while bathing, just drain the water and replace it with a fresh one and continue soaking it. As a matter of fact, bathing is also a form of exercise for these leathery creatures.

How often and how long do I need to bathe my iguana?

If they're still young, you could start easing them into it and gradually lengthen their bathing time as they get older. 30 minutes is ideal for adult iguanas. You can bathe or soak your pet every day if you can or at least once a week to ensure that your iguana maintains a good hygiene.

Important Reminder when bathing your iguana:

- Never leave your pet alone or unsupervised in a bathtub or wherever you will clean/bathe them.
- Make sure the water is at proper temperature, not too hot or too cold.
- Make your bathtub iguana – proof.

Do I need to trim my pet's claws?

It's ideal to regularly trim your iguana's claws. This is actually more beneficial for you as the owner because most owners usually have suffered from severe scratches due to untrimmed claws. Being scratched or punctured by iguanas especially large species can be very dangerous plus they can also ruin some of your household stuff.

How often should I trim my iguana's claws?

The length of the claws depends on how rapid your pet is actually growing. You can opt to trim it once every 2 – 3 weeks especially when it's still young. As it gets older though, you just need to trim it at least once a month since growth rate slows down at this point.

Why is it important to keep the cage humid or misted?

It simply helps whenever they're shedding. If you want to create a more humid enclosure, you can mist it twice a day whenever it's time for your pet to shed or you can use fogging equipment or misting fixtures to make it automatic. Some keepers also provide a moist box for their pet during the shedding period. This could be a container that is cover with moist moss.

Importance of Shedding

Reptiles including iguanas shed in patches not as a whole piece of skin. Don't ever try to peel off the skin because it will naturally shed on its own, peeling could be really painful for your pet.

Iguanas shed around four to six weeks or more often than that especially if the environment has the right temperature and humidity levels. Most iguanas have an easier time shedding because the environment is right, and they have access to bodies of water.

Shedding is needed because it enables them to grow a new layer of covering, just like with humans, our dry skin cells are constantly replace whenever we take a bath and scrub our bodies, of course, reptiles cannot be groomed per se which is why this is their natural way of doing it. Once the new skin forms, it will begin to separate from the old layer, and it will eventually fall off into patches.

Chapter Eight: Sexing Your Iguanas

Before you expect baby iguanas you must first learn the gender of your pets otherwise if they're both of the same sex, you'll be disappointed because at the end of the day, nothing "exotic" could come out of it. Once you found out your pets' gender you can then set up the right breeding conditions and wait for their "breeding season." Most of them is ready for mating at some point each year, but of course the time will vary depending on each species. What you can do to prepare as an owner is to determine the signs that your pet/s is ready for breeding so that you know what to expect before, during, and after the mating season. This chapter will help you learn about breeding iguanas.

Male vs. Female Iguanas – Sexual Dimorphism

The sex of your iguana cannot be determined at an early age (although you may already see some physical traits), you'll only know it until they reach their sexual maturity. It's hard to distinguish a male from a female iguana especially if they're still at young or juvenile stage which means that these creatures are not sexually dimorphic. How do you know if your pet already reaches sexual maturity? Well, unlike most creatures, iguanas maturity is determine by its size and not the age.

Usually, if the male iguana reaches about 6 inch SVL some of them are already prepared to mate, for females though most of them would have to reach at least 10 inch SVL before being able to breed. Your pets can be sexually matured after about 1 ½ to 2 years.

Identifying the Sex

Here are some physical signs that your pet iguana is either a male or female species:

Male Iguanas:

- Large jaw muscles on both sides of the iguana's lower jaw or sometimes called jowls.
- Blocky and big - looking head

- Has fatty deposits on the forehead
- Has large scales on both sides of the head and in the chin area
- Have longer dorsal spikes compared to females
- Has large pores in the innermost part of its thigh that excretes a waxy substance
- Has a bulging tail because this is where the hemipenis is located (you'll only see it once they're breeding already).
- Generally have larger and bulkier body size than females.

Female Iguanas:

- Has smaller heads
- Doesn't have fatty or bulks around the head/eyes
- Lacks large jowls
- Also has femoral pores (but are smaller) on its thigh and it also lacks the waxy substance
- Have a smaller but longer body structure
- Doesn't have protruding or bulge on its tail since they don't possess a hemipenis.

'Tis the Season for Breeding!

Males and females undergo physical and behavioral changes once they are ready to mate. As the owner (especially if you're thinking about breeding them) you may want to take note of such changes so that you'll be prepared for the breeding season as well. You may need to give them a space where they can freely roam and breed without being stressed out aside from that you may need to also do some changes on their diet especially when females are already beginning to ovulate. It's also imperative that you give them a place to dig around because that's what female species do when they're ovulating; they're trying to find a place where they can lay their eggs.

Here are the physical and behavioral changes in both males and females that you should take note of especially when they entered the breeding season or have reached sexual maturity.

Physical Changes for Male Species:

- The coloring of their skin turns to orange
- The pores in their thighs becomes enlarged

- Presence of sperm plugs (appears as orange or creamed colored substance) or sometimes a fresh semen which resembles like a melted cheese.

Behavioral Changes for Male Species:

Owners usually have a tougher time dealing with male iguanas during the mating season which is why you must learn to deal with them especially when they reached maturity. They could be more difficult to handle and can also be more aggressive and dangerous so be very cautious. Although some male species remain docile, it's always better to keep your guard up and not "mess" with it (at least for the breeding period). Below are the behavioral signs to look out for:

- Increased and rapid head bobbing
- Increased territory roaming (or a tendency to be more territorially defensive)
- Unpredictable attacks to other creature or to the owner even if they've previously formed a bond
- Appetite may decrease
- You may find them courting or chasing after female species (which can tend to be very aggressive acts but that's normal for them)

- May become dehydrated due to appetite loss (so it's important you mist their enclosure/cage or also add humidity, you can also feed them small amounts of watery fruits)
- Tends to forget toilet habits because of their "breeding hormones" (but the habits will kick in again once the breeding season is over)
- Wild or aggressive mating instincts (they will literally try to mate with anything including their female owners so be very cautious)

<u>Important Reminders:</u>

- During breeding season male iguanas may also stalk their female owners in attempt to mate with them or their legs. This is especially for those female owners that are on their period, their male iguana pets may have mating instincts at them so be very careful when interacting with them.

- What you can do to perhaps lessen such aggressive behaviors is to provide a plush toy for them to "mate" on like a stuffed animal. It can serve as an outlet for them especially during breeding season.

Physical Changes for Female Species:

- Female iguanas will start to develop eggs in her ovaries (this applies even if she hasn't mated with any male species).
- Their skin in their legs and belly may turn to orange just like in males (though most do not).
- Loss of appetite (making them slimmer – looking)
- Has bulge bellies due to production of eggs

Behavioral Changes for Female Species:

Your females can lay eggs even if no male species has mated with them. If your female gets fertilized without the act of mating that means they are "gravid." The problem with being gravid is that your pet may have high risk of MBD or Metabolic Bone disease especially if they're not provided with enough calcium. Keepers of gravid female iguanas usually add calcium or water – rich fruits to their pet's food especially during breeding season. Perhaps the only behavioral change that is noticeable among females is that you'll often see them digging or burrowing a "nesting spot."

This act of digging is natural instinct because that's what these animals do in the while if they are ready to lay their eggs anytime soon. Females will constantly search for a nesting place in the forest but since they are in captivity, they might resort to just burrowing everything inside the cage or in your backyard. Make sure that your home is iguana – proof to avoid things being destroyed or causing injuries to your pet.

What you can do to accommodate this behavior is to simply provide a nesting box like a durable plastic box or sandbox. Fill it up with soil so that it will serve as their sort of "cave" where they can safely lay their eggs when the time comes. You need to make sure that they have adequate places to burrow in because if not they may tend to withhold laying their eggs which can be dangerous for their health once the egg hatches inside their bellies.

Breeding Process

- Once you see physical and behavioral changes in both your male or female species that means they are ready to mate or go into the process of egg development (as with the case of gravid females).

- You'll usually see the male courting the female or aggressively stalking or chasing her.

- Males will usually grab the female and bite it in the neck or scale area above the female's head to have a grip on her or hold her into position. They will try to mount the female so expect that there will be scratching and biting as well as aggressive behaviors because the females will seem to look like they're resisting the males at first.

- When the male and female is finally in the mating position, you'll see that their tails are intertwined, that's when the male's hemipenis will come out to penetrate the female.

- Mating usually lasts about 10 – 15 minutes or more. Both creatures do not make any sounds as they mate, and once they're finish they'll just take a quick rest, and go on roaming around again.

For gravid females, you'll know if the eggs are already developed when you can already feel it under your pet's belly. Just do it gently so as not to crack any eggs inside as that could be dangerous for your pet. The egg laying and production will occur every year even if they mate with a male or not, but as mentioned earlier, the period of egg production can vary depending on the individual species.

It's very important to also take your female iguana to the vet for an X – ray examination before and after egg laying to make sure that the eggs are fully developed and to prevent any unlaid eggs as it could be dangerous for the iguana's health.

Incubation and Hatching Quick Facts

- Green Iguana: average eggs in a clutch is 20 to 70
- Blue Iguana: average eggs in a clutch is 5 – 20
- Incubation Period: 90 to 120 days
- Average Eggs Size: 15 mm (diameter); 35 to 40 mm (length)

Chapter Nine: Health Issues of Iguanas

In this chapter, we will take a look at some illness that is very common among iguana species in general so that you can prevent them from getting sick and also keep them healthy. You'll learn what causes such diseases or disorders and also have an idea on how to treat them if such things happen. This is also beneficial so that you can take preventive measures. As with other pets or creatures whether they are reptiles or mammals, the key in keeping your pet away from diseases is adequate environmental condition and right diet. If you maintain the cleanliness of their cage or enclosures, provide them with all their basic physical and territorial needs, and feed them with nutritious food they'll surely be not just healthy but also happy iguanas!

Common Minor Illness

Parasite Infestations

Parasite infestation is very common among iguanas and other reptile species. It can also be associated with other illnesses because parasites also serve as vectors for other disease causing agents like bacteria that cause pneumonia and infectious stomatitis which is why it's important to identify the parasites as soon as possible so that proper treatment can be given.

Parasite infestation is mainly because of unsanitary living conditions, imports, and improper husbandry. These creatures are usually found on pets imported from other countries that are not properly quarantined or may not be quarantined at all.

Causes:

Parasites are usually acquired from ingesting an infected or contaminated feeder as well as infected feces from other animals. These parasites are microscopic and therefore can't be seen by the naked eye, that's why you need to bring in a fresh fecal sample for laboratory analysis.

Parasites sucks blood from its host and can be potentially life – threatening if there's already a swarm of mites or ticks in your pet iguana which could eventually cause loss of blood. Aside from that, these parasites can also transfer a disease from one animal species to another enabling other bacterial or viral diseases enter your pet's bloodstream.

Symptoms:

The usual signs of intestinal parasites are smelly feces, lethargy, weight loss, and lack of appetite as well as vomiting. If you notice your pet having a dull - looking appearance it might already be infested with mites. You should check areas around its eyes, its cloaca or its underbelly because this is where most parasites accumulate.

Treatment:

Usually deworming medications are prescribed but of course, it will still depend on the kind of parasite living inside your iguana. A fecal sample is taken to find eggs of the parasites, however sometimes worms don't shed eggs so a negative fecal test doesn't necessarily mean that your pet is free from parasites. Several fecal tests or samples should be submitted.

Tips for Prevention:

- You have to spot clean and thoroughly treat the entire enclosure or shelter of your pets.

- If you have more than one or two iguana, parasites could be difficult to remove if not prevented so you better quarantined them beforehand.

- Make sure that even after your iguana is free of these mites or ticks their enclosure is free of it completely because if the environment is not properly cleaned or treated, parasites can potentially accumulate and infest your pet again.

Metabolic Bone Disease (MBD)

Gravid female iguana species are prone to MBD! This disease is caused by a lack in dietary calcium, improper lighting, and also imbalanced nutrition.

If the calcium levels are low, the body will be forced to get calcium source straight from the bones so that there will be enough energy for the body to function especially for muscle movements and metabolism. The effect, however is that the bones become weak and eventually brittle.

Symptoms:

The usual signs you should look out for is bent leg bones, double elbows, stunted growth, decrease in the use of its tongue, double knees, misaligned mouth, soft or if it's grabbing its own limbs or head.

Treatment:

If your pet iguana gets affected with metabolic bone disease it cannot be reversed. However, the process of progression of the disease can be stopped. If prevented, the bones can be treated with proper medications, and it can heal over time.

Tips for Prevention:

- Proper husbandry such as enough access to UVB lighting as well as proper nutrition can correct the calcium imbalance in the body.

- For gravid females, you should make sure that you provide them with proper amounts of calcium. You can sprinkle their food with supplements to aid during their egg development period, prevent binding of eggs and also lessen the risk of MBD.

Gout

Gout is simply the inflammation of the iguana's joints that can make your pet experience mobility issues. The main cause of gout in iguanas is excess protein. When there's excess protein that means that the body will have a hard time absorbing all of it. The proteins that are not properly absorbed then turns into uric acid, and this uric acid hardens up and forms into acid crystals that are lodge into other organs like the kidney, liver, lungs and joints. Another reason why crystals form in the body is because of dehydration or sometimes damaged kidneys. If kidneys are damaged, the food/acid in the stomach will not be properly filtered and could also promote buildup of such uric acid.

Symptoms:

Signs of gout in iguanas include swollen limbs and organs particularly the eyes, painful joints, lethargy, dull or unhealthy scales and mobility issues. If you see your pet having a hard time crawling or climbing unlike how it used to before, it could be a sign that their joints are aching.

Treatment:

If you see signs of gout, it's imperative that you bring your pet to the vet immediately. If it's not properly treated, the buildup of crystals can continue and may cause disability to your iguana or it can also be fatal. Usually surgery or medication is done to iguanas that have gout plus changes in diet and husbandry. However, there's no permanent cure for gout, so management and prevention is necessary.

Tips for Prevention:

- Make sure you are feeding your pet with the right diet.

- Consult with your vet on the ratio of protein that is suitable for your pet so that you'll have an idea on the amount that should be fed.

- Make sure that you encourage your iguana to drink huge amounts of water every day. Water helps in flushing out excess toxic in the body and also aids in digestion and prevents crystal formations due to uric acid.

Goiter

Goiter just like in mammals and humans occur when there are low amounts of iodine in the body. It is the thyroid glands job to produce such hormones in order to regulate metabolism, shedding, energy level, mood and also growth of an iguana. If there isn't enough iodine in the body, the thyroid gland located in the neck area will swell up and will eventually produce low levels of hormones thus decreasing metabolism, stumping growth, and make the iguana dull and lethargic. The iguana can also lose their appetite making it more prone to other diseases.

The main cause of goiter is that there are high levels of goitrogens in the food of your iguana. These are chemicals that usually affect the system's ability to properly utilize iodine. Foods that contain goitrogens are broccoli, kale, brussel sprouts, cabbage and cauliflower so make sure to only feed it to them in moderation.

Symptoms:

Symptoms of goiter include swollen neck, swollen body, inactivity, slow growth, changes in temperament due to lack of energy.

Treatment:

There's actually no medication or procedure that will treat the development of goiter, the vet may recommend iodine supplements but most likely you'll be advised to change the diet of your pet by either lessening or completely eliminating foods that contains high levels of goitrogen.

Tips for Prevention:

- Ensure that your pet is getting proper amounts of veggies and fruits. Too much or too little is always bad. The key is that everything should be in moderation and also variety.

- Study, do research or ask your vet about the appropriate amounts of food or certain vegetables to avoid such illnesses.

Treatment for Injuries

This section will give you an idea on how to deal with common cuts, wounds and even broken limbs. It's important to note however that all the tips here will only serve as your first aid. If you think the wound or cuts are getting worse and would need more than just a first aid, it's best to bring your pet to the veterinarian for proper treatment.

Tips in treating cuts or minor flesh wounds:

- Do not panic if your pet accidentally cut himself or becomes injured for some reason. Stay calm so that you can think and act better.
- Make sure to assess the situation before doing or applying anything. If you think the wound needs more than just a first aid, don't hesitate to bring it to the vet.
- Assess the wound and see where it's coming from. If too much blood is already wasted don't waste time and just bring your pet to the nearest clinic.
- If the wound or cut is non – fatal, what you can do is to soak the injured part in water mixed with Betadine to aid in clotting. You can also spray the wounded part with medications similar to Betadine.

- After doing that, cover the injured area with gauze or bandage to prevent it from being infected.

Tips in dealing with broken limbs:

- Again, do not panic, speak calmly and try to also keep your pet as relaxed as possible.
- Do not try to straighten out or cast the broken limb! Very gently and slowly move him from wherever he is to prevent further damage.
- You need to bring him to the vet immediately, and keep the animal as immobile as possible.
- Move him to a flat or stable surface and support its body while you're transporting or transferring him.
- The vet will take an X – ray of the broken limb and will give your pet some anesthesia as well. They will then cast the limb and fix what's broken.
- All reptiles and amphibians have a hard time healing so you can expect your pet to have a slow recovery after he/she experiences a broken bone/s.
- Follow the vet's orders and avoid any strenuous activities for your pet.
- A pain reliever or some medication may be prescribed for your iguana. Make sure to ask the effects of it so that you'll know what to expect.

Chapter Ten: Care Sheet and Summary

The right diet, good husbandry and breeding practices as well as knowledge about your iguana's behaviors can help you provide the best living condition for this wild and exotic but beautiful looking creature. This chapter will give you a quick summary of all the essential things you need to remember when it comes to taking care of your iguana. Always remember that the wellness and happiness of your pet depends on how well you take care of all their needs and how well you form a bond with them. That is the key to having a healthy, happy and loving relationship with your pet iguana. Have fun!

Biological Information

Distribution and Range: Central America, Southern Mexico, and South America

Breed Size: small to medium sized breed

Body Type and Appearance: They display a stocky stature; they have saggy skin found on their throats; their spine runs along their head, neck, back, and tail.

Length: 3 to 6 feet

Weight: Weighs an average of 4 to 8 kilos

Skin Texture: scaly texture

Color: Their colors depend on the specie they belong. In general they have green, yellow, and brown color.

Temperament: They are docile and easy to take care of; they can also be territorial especially the males

Diet: They feed on different kinds of insects, fruits and leaves

Habitat: Lowland tropical forest on which they have access to water to deserted places depending on which specie they belong

Health Conditions: Generally healthy but predisposed to common illnesses such as egg binding, metabolic bone disease, burns, dehydration, shedding, and respiratory infections

Lifespan: They can live an average life of 15 to 20 years

<u>**Sub - Species**</u>

Genus Cyclura - Rock Iguanas
Distribution: West India

Physical characteristics:

Length: 5 feet

Body: Its body color varies. They can be gray, green, blue, brown or even bright red.

Genus Amblyrhyncus - Marine Iguana
Distribution: Rocky waters and mangroves found in Galapagos Islands

Physical characteristics:

Length: 3 to 5 feet

Body: They exhibit a reddish coloration that resembles a mixture of jagged rocks and coral reef.

Genus Conolophus - Land Iguanas

Distribution: Galapagos Islands

Physical characteristics:

Length: 3 to 5 feet

Body: Their colors range between brown, yellow, red, and dark gray

Genus Ctenosauria - Spiny Tailed Iguanas

Distribution: Mexico and Central America

Physical characteristics:

Length: 5 inches to 4 feet

Body: They have spiny scales found in their back and tail. Their colors range from orange, green, brown, bright yellow, and gray.

Genus Dipsosaurus- Desert Iguanas

Distribution: Mexico and Southwestern United States

Physical characteristics:

Length: 16 inches

Body: They have the capacity to change color from gray to white

Genus Sauromalus- Chuckwalla

Distribution: Northern Mexico ad Southwestern United States

Physical characteristics:-

Length: 15 to 30 inches

Iguanas as Pets

Body: Males are usually covered in red or orange color while the females have yellowish spots or gray found on their backs

Iguanas as Pets

- Expect that during the first days, the iguana will look afraid as there is a tendency that it will feel intimidated by its owner's size.
- Do not get frustrated if this happens since it is just natural. Wait until your pet has fully adjusted.
- Have yourself familiarized by visiting your pet's enclosure every day. If properly socialized, they can get along well with other animals as well as other people besides its owner.
- Iguanas can be territorial especially the male ones. They may display head bobbing, hissing, and tail twitching as signs that they are being defensive. They may try to compress their body laterally in order for to look taller and intimidating.
- If you're going to introduce a smaller pet like bird, beware of potential aggression that your iguana might display as they are really against small intruders. Each introduction will be different as pet varies from each other.

- You should gather all the information you need in order to be well educated with regard to the pet you want to have.
- You should be able to answer generic questions like how much will it cost, how big will it get, what kind of food does it eat, what kind of care does it require, etc.
- Do not immediately drop the news that you want an iguana as a pet especially if the members of your family are uptight with this idea.

Major Pros:
- Its food is easy to find as an iguana has a herbivore diet which means they feed on plants, vegetables, and fruits alone.

- This specie can get along well with other animals.

Major Cons:
- Iguanas can be quite aggressive.

- Taking an exotic animal to the vet will cost you more than taking a dog or a cat to the vet.

Licensing

- Appendix II is a list of species that are not necessarily threatened with extinction now but the probability of it depends on how closely controlled the trade is. This is where iguana belongs.

- In general, you don't need to have approval from wildlife organizations or authorities in order to have your iguana licensed. All you have to do is to provide a document with the name, identity of the specie on which your pet belongs.

Costs

Purchase price of iguana: $30 to $100 above

The costs of iguanas depend on its size, age, specie, and the place where you bought it. You may expect the amount of $30 to $100 and more for an iguana being sold by a reputable breeder, in general.

Enclosure: $90 or more

Iguanas can grow as large as 6 feet when they reach adulthood. You must ensure that the enclosure you'll be purchasing is large enough for all the habitat necessities with a remaining free space for your pet to roam around.

Substrate: $10 to $20

Make sure that you'll be able to provide the best kind of substrate for your pet. You can use paper towels, alfalfa pellets, and wrapping paper.

Cage Accessories: $10 to $25

You may add cage decors such as branches, leaves, live plants, and other things that would make the cage pleasing to the eyes.

Food: $15 above

Iguanas feed on plants, vegetables, and fruits.

Veterinary Care: $75 to $100 or more

It is advisable for your pet to visit the vet once in a while for a routine check-up in order to make sure that its health is exceptional.

Lighting and Heating Equipment: $100 or more

Iguanas are in need of UV radiation specifically UVA and UVB.

How to Acquire an Iguana

<u>Where to Acquire Iguanas:</u>

Private breeders

- Private breeders are the ones taking care of the iguanas personally therefore you'll be able to see if they are reputable or not depending on how the iguanas are being raised

Reptile Shop

- You may find a variety of iguanas here compared to other commercial pet stores. It means that you'll have more options to choose from

Reptile shows

- You can buy a healthy iguana with a cheaper price. This is ideal especially if your budget is limited

- You can meet different reptile owners and enthusiasts

Local Rescue Center

- You can have a fully grown iguana without the need of enduring its growing years

- You can give a new home to those that have been abandoned by their past owners

Characteristics of a Reputable Iguana Breeder

- He must be knowledgeable about iguanas and must be able to give information that is not common.

- He should be able to give you some points on how to take care of it

- He should be friendly as a reputable breeder builds a good relationship

- He should ask you questions about yourself as a legit breeder wants to know if he is also dealing with a person who's willing and able to take care of an iguana.
- He should be patient.

Habitat Needs of Your Iguana:

Cage Size

- When buying a cage, the first thing you have to consider is the size of it.
- You should realize that iguanas can grow as long as 6 feet when they reach adulthood.
- You must ensure that the enclosure you'll be purchasing is large enough for all the habitat necessities with a free space for your pet to roam around.

Cage Material

- Make sure that the enclosure you will purchase or build is either made out of thick plywood or thick glass/ Plexiglass

Cage Safety

- Make sure that the enclosure you'll be providing for your pet has lids and safety latches on it to prevent them from going out of their cage.

Substrate

- Choosing the right substrate is essential in maintaining the comfort as well as the humidity inside the cage.
- Provide a thick layer of substrate for your pet's enclosure.

Spag Moss/Plants

- For a large enclosure, you may use two to three bags of it.
- This is essential for absorbing moisture to prevent molds from accumulating inside the enclosure.

Water Bowls

- Make sure that the size of the water bowl is appropriate for the size of your pet.

Types of Lighting/Heating Equipment

- **Fluorescent Tubes** - This is the most accessible type of UV lamp or bulb.

- **Mercury Vapor Lamps** - This looks like incandescent bulbs. It is a new way to provide UVB for your pet.

<u>Humidity</u>

- Iguanas need high humidity inside their enclosure. The proper level of humidity they require is between 65% and 75%.

The Right Diet for Your Iguana

- In general their diet consists of fibrous plants. Iguanas don't eat much fruit in the wild but since it's in captivity, it's also recommended that you feed it with a healthy amount of fruits once in a while.

- Vegetables should make up 40 - 45% of your iguana's diet while fruits should make up 10% or less, and should be fed no more than twice a week.

- The rule of thumb when you're feeding your iguana a veggie diet is: the more varied the better.

- You need to cut the veggies and fruits in bite – size pieces, other pet owners like to grate it or chop it finely.

- If you bought a lot of veggies that's about good for a week or so, you can place the excess veggies in a zip lock bag and place it in the freezer, then just pop it in the microwave.

- Feeding your pet iguana should be done daily. You can feed it either 2 to 3 times a day. Just make sure you feed them daily so that they'll stay healthy.
- When it comes to the amount, it highly depends on the age, the size and even the appetite of the iguana.

- It's best to remove it so as not to risk eating rotten food and maintain the cage's cleanliness.

Body Language of Iguanas

- **Dewlap Display:** The dewlap is the iguana's flap on both sides of its head or neck area. They're greeting you or trying to impress their potential mate. It's also a sign of territoriality.
- **Bobbing of Head:** If the species are bobbing rapidly, it can mean that they are feeling aggressive or agitated especially the males, so better exercise caution and don't approach them as much as possible if ever they're feeling an extreme form of irritation.

- **Flicking of Tongue:** Flicking of tongue among reptiles is a sign that they're trying to get more information about their environment or occurrence. They use it to make sense of their surroundings, to check out its water or food before eating it, to sense people, and other strange object as well.
- **Tail Whip:** It usually means that it's being threatened or showing some form of aggression because that's what they usually use as first defense or as a weapon against potential threats.
- **Squirming:** If your pet is squirming, it most likely means that it's not comfortable with being handled.
- **Sneezing:** It's simply trying to get rid of their body salt. It's not also a sign of lung infection but you may need to adjust its diet if you notice the sneezes going too far or worse.
- **Hatchet Mode:** It means that they are either intimidated or aggressive, you'll see if it's standing up, while it is wagging its tail or even have an extended dewlap.
- **Digging Up:** If you see your pet digging up, it's usually a sign she is pregnant or would lay eggs in the near future.

Grooming and Maintenance Guidelines

- Regular cleaning prevents the possible transmission of diseases which can be found in the fecal matter of reptiles, and which may be transmissible to humans.
- Spot cleaning the interior of the cage should be done as often as possible at once every other day.
- During the cleaning process, you will need to relocate the iguana so that you can clean and sterilize the entire tank components such as its hiding spots, substrate, plants/branches etc.
- The water bowls should also be replaced more than once a week to prevent bacterial growth.
- Soaking can also help in their shedding process as well as brush off any food stains or feces.
- Make sure to wash your hands thoroughly, and use antibacterial soap.
- It's ideal to regularly trim your iguana's claws. You can opt to trim it once every 2 – 3 weeks especially when it's still young.
- If you want to create a more humid enclosure, you can mist it twice a day whenever it's time for your pet to shed or you can use fogging equipment or misting fixtures to make it automatic. Never leave your pet alone or unsupervised in a bathtub or wherever you will clean/bathe them.

- Make sure the water is at proper temperature, not too hot or too cold.

Sexing Your Iguanas

Male Iguanas:

- Large jaw muscles on both sides of the iguana's lower jaw or sometimes called jowls.
- Blocky and big - looking head
- Has fatty deposits on the forehead
- Has large scales on both sides of the head and in the chin area
- Have longer dorsal spikes compared to females

Female Iguanas:

- Has smaller heads
- Doesn't have fatty or bulks around the head/eyes
- Lacks large jowls
- Have a smaller but longer body structure

Breeding Season Changes:

Physical Changes for Male Species:

- The coloring of their skin turns to orange

- The pores in their thighs becomes enlarged
- Presence of sperm plugs or sometimes a fresh semen

Behavioral Changes for Male Species:

- Increased and rapid head bobbing
- Increased territory roaming
- Appetite may decrease
- You may find them courting or chasing after female species

Physical Changes for Female Species:

- Female iguanas will start to develop eggs in her ovaries
- Has bulge bellies due to production of eggs
- Loss of appetite (making them slimmer – looking)

Behavioral Changes for Female Species:

- You'll often see them digging or burrowing a nesting spot.

Incubation and Hatching

- Green Iguana: average eggs in a clutch is 20 to 70
- Blue Iguana: average eggs in a clutch is 5 – 20
- Incubation Period: 90 to 120 days

- Average Eggs Size: 15 mm (diameter); 35 to 40 mm (length)

Health Issues

- Parasite Infestations
- Metabolic Bone Disease (MBD)
- Gout
- Goiter

Treatment for Injuries

Tips in treating cuts or minor flesh wounds:

- Make sure to assess the situation before doing or applying anything. If you think the wound needs more than just a first aid, don't hesitate to bring it to the vet.

- Assess the wound and see where it's coming from. If too much blood is already wasted don't waste time and just bring your pet to the nearest clinic.

- If the wound or cut is non – fatal, what you can do is to soak the injured part in water mixed with Betadine to aid in clotting. You can also spray the wounded part with medications similar to Betadine.

Tips in dealing with broken limbs:

- Do not try to straighten out or cast the broken limb! Very gently and slowly move him from wherever he is to prevent further damage.

- You need to bring him to the vet immediately, and keep the animal as immobile as possible.

- Move him to a flat or stable surface and support its body while you're transporting or transferring him.

Glossary of Iguana Terms

Acclimate - The process of being accustomed, comfortable, an get used to something

Arboreal - Species living in trees. Wild Iguanas are considered arboreal as they spend most of their time feeding on leaves in trees

Alligator Roll - A behavior displayed by Iguanas when they desperately want to let go whenever they are being held by leash or hands

Aloe Vera - A substance in gel-like form produced in the stems of Aloe Vera plants. This is often used as a lubricant to aid in shedding.

Analgesic - A type of drug that relieves pain. It can be injectable, topical, or oral

ARAV - Association of Reptile and Amphibian Veterinarians.

Bask - Lying under sun in order to absorb its heat and UV rays

Betadine - An iodine solution that is utilized to clean wounds

Brewer's Yeast- A type of dietary supplement with inactivated yeast cells that is rich in vitamin B1 or thiamine

Bug eyes - This is also referred to as frog eyes. It is a way to describe the behavior of iguanas on which their eyes are "bugged out" or puffed up and closed

Ca:P - used to conote teh ratio between Calcium and Phosphorus

Calcium - A mineral produced by leafy green vegetables and other foods, it is vital for building strong bones.

CHE - Ceramic Heat Emitter

Cloaca - Another term for vent

Cold – blooded - It also means ectothermic

Crocodile Roll - Same with Alligator Roll

Cruciferous - It refers to the vegetables belonging in the cabbage family such as kale, cabbage, and broccoli

Dehydration - A condition on which the body lacks proper amount of water

Dewlap- A flap of the skin found under the chin

Digits - Term used for fingers or toes

Disinfect - A treatment to kill or inhibit the growth of microorganisms mainly bacteria

Dystocia - Similar with Egg-Binding

Ectothermic - The inability to heat the own body from body

Egg-Bound - Female iguanas suffering from a condition on which the eggs are retained inside their body and are enable to lay them.

Enclosure - Another term used for cage or habitat

Evil-eye - A term to describe the intense or angry look of iguanas when they are displeased

Femoral Pores - Pores that are found along the inner thigh on the hind legs of iguanas

Fibrous Osteodystrophy - Another term used to denote Metabolic Bone Disease

Fluorescent Bulbs- A long tubular light bulb that contains phosphor

Free Roaming - Allowing the Iguana to roam around the house

Frog Eyes - Similar with Bug Eyes

Full Spectrum- A type of fluorescent bulb which gives off light similar to real sunlight

Gaping - When an iguana opens its mouth and holds it.

Glycerin - A type of substance used as a lubricant

Goiter- A condition on which the thyroid gland is swollen

Goitrogens - Chemical compounds that inhibits the body to absorb and use iodine

Gravid - It is when female iguanas are carrying either fertile or infertile eggs

Gravidity - The condition of carrying eggs

Habitat - Similar with enclosure

Hardware Cloth - A wire screen material used to make iguana enclosures

Hatchet Mode - It is when an iguana flattens its body from side to side

Head Bob - The form of communication iguanas practice

Heliothermic - Process of absorbing heat and energy from the sun

Hemipenes - A male's organ used for copulation

Herbivore - An animal that feeds on plants

Herp - Abbreviation used for Herpetile

Herp Vet - A veterinarian that specializes in taking care of herpetiles or reptiles and amphibians

Herpetile - Refers to reptiles and amphibians

Herpetoculturist - A person who breeds or owns herpetiles

Herpetologist - A person who studies reptiles and amphibians

Hindgut - A section of an iguana's intestine found between the small and large intestine

Humidifier- An appliance that emits water vapor

Humidity- The measure of the presence of water in the air

Husbandry- It means the care of something

Hygiene- It means cleanliness of something

Hyperthyroidism- It is when the thyroid gland cannot produce enough hormones responsible for regulating metabolism

Hysterectomy- A surgical procedure removing the ovaries, oviducts, or uterus

Iglet- A juvenile iguana

Impaction- Blockage in the intestine

Incandescent bulbs- Socket-type light bulbs used as light and heat source

Infrared bulbs- Light bulbs that give off infrared wavelengths and visible light

Internet Mesh™- netting that is flexible used in making an iguana enclosure

Intravenous (IV) - A term used to define injections

Jacobson's Organ- Also known as vomeronasal organ

Jowl- The skin and muscle found under the lower jawbone

Kwik-Stop- A brand of styptic powder

KY Jelly- A lubricant utilized for loosening stuck shed

Lethargy- A condition on which the activity level is low

Love toy- An object used as an outlet for sexual urges and aggressions of iguanas during the breeding season

MBD- Metabolic Bone Disease

Mineral Oil- Used to treat constipation and loosen stuck shed

Mites- Small external parasites infesting iguanas

Mouth Rot- Also known as stomatitis or ulcerative stomatitis

Necropsy- Term to define animal autopsy

Neuter- Removal of testes surgically

Nolvasan- A brand of chlorhexidine diacetate disinfectant

Nose Rub- A common wound obtained by iguanas when they rub their nose against something

Nuchal Crest- The top part of the neck

Oxalates- Chemicals found naturally in some plants

Parasites- Organisms that survive by living in or on another organism

Parietal Eye- A transparent scale located in the top of the head able to detect light and dark

Particulate- Particles often small in size

Per Os (PO) - It means to give orally

Phosphorus- A mineral found in different food

Phytates- Chemicals found in some plants.

Plexigals- A clear and lightweight material used for setting up cages

Posturing- A term used to define iguanas displaying aggression

Prolapse- When an internal organ protrudes and stays outside the body.

Protein- Molecules built from amino acids

Protozoans- Single-celled organisms

Renal- A term to define kidneys

Rut- It means breeding season

Quick- The blood vessels and nerves at the center of the toenail or claw

Saline- A salt water solution

Salmonella - A bacteria that causes fever, nausea, and diarrhea. This causes salmonellosis

Salt Expulsion- The process of eradicating salt by snorting it out through the nostrils

Secondary Nutritional Hyoparathyroidism - Metabolic Bone Disease

Semen Plug- similar to sperm plug

Shudder Bob- A rapid side-to-side movements of the head

Sperm Plug- Packets of sperm produced by iguanas

Spikes- Projections displayed along the back of an iguana

Sterilize- The process of completely destroying bacteria and other microorganisms found in a non-living object

STL- Snout Tail Length

Somatitis- Similar with Mouth Rot

Subcutaneous (SC)- It means under the skin

Substrate- A thing lining the bottom of an enclosure

Subtympanic Scale- A slightly cone-shaped scale found under the lower jaw

Thermoregulate- The process of regulating body temperature

Thiamin- Another term for Vitamin B1

Third Eye- Similar with Parietal Eye

Tongue Flick- It is when the iguana extends its tongue into the air or onto and object

Toxic- Things that is poisonous or hazardous to the health

Tube lights- Another term for UV fluorescent light bulbs

Tuberculate Scales- A pyramid-shaped scales found along the side of the neck

Tympanum- Ear drum

Ulcerative Stomatitis- Another term for Mouth Rot

Ultraviolet light (UV light) - Wavelengths of light that are shorter than visible light waves essential for an iguana's enclosure

Urates- Semi-solid part of the waste

Vent- Opening for the digestive, urinary, and reproductive systems

Vitamin D3- Vitamin that can be obtained through exposure to UV light

Vomeronasal Organ- Similar to Jacobson's Organ

Worms- Long cylindrical animal

Index

D

E

F

G

H

Iguanas as Pets

I

M

N

O

P

R

S

T

U

V

W

Y

Photo Credits

https://pixabay.com/en/iguana-lizard-green-exotic-reptile-2880916/

Page 81 Photo by user Stevepb via Pixabay.com, https://pixabay.com/en/iguana-reptile-lizard-dragon-385016/

Page 93 Photo by user Pexels via Pixabay.com, https://pixabay.com/en/animal-close-up-exotic-iguana-1851145/

References

Behavior of the Green Iguana – PetEducation.com
http://www.peteducation.com/article.cfm?c=17+1796&aid=3589

Body Language – Green Iguana Society
http://www.greenigsociety.org/body.htm

Breeding Iguanas – Reptile Magazine
http://www.reptilesmagazine.com/Breeding-Iguanas/

Cage & Habitat – Pet Iguana Care
http://petiguanacare.org/cage-habitat/

Glossary of Iguana Terms – Green Iguana Society
http://www.greenigsociety.org/glossary.htm

Habitat Basics – Green Iguana Society
http://www.greenigsociety.org/habitatbasics.htm

Heat, Lighting & Humidity – Green Iguana Society
http://www.greenigsociety.org/heatlighthumidity.htm

How to Clean & Disinfect Reptile Cages – PetEducation.com
http://www.peteducation.com/article.cfm?aid=2847

Food & Diet – Pet Iguana Care
http://petiguanacare.org/food-diet/

Giving an Iguana A Bath – Dummies.com
http://www.dummies.com/pets/reptiles/giving-an-iguana-a-bath/

Green Iguana – National Geographic
https://www.nationalgeographic.com/animals/reptiles/g/green-iguana/

Green Iguana – Wikipedia.org
https://en.wikipedia.org/wiki/Green_iguana

Green Iguana Care Sheet – Reptiles Magazine
http://www.reptilesmagazine.com/Care-Sheets/Lizards/Green-Iguana/

Health & Illness – Pet Iguana Care
http://petiguanacare.org/health-illness/

Iguana – Pet Iguana Care
http://petiguanacare.org/

Into The Iguana: Potential Behavior & Attitudes of the Iguana – Today's Planet
http://www.todaysplanet.com/pg/beta/lizardlover/page19.htm

Keeping Iguanas as Pets – Reptile Expert UK
http://www.reptileexpert.co.uk/keepingiguanasaspets.html

Taming - Pet Iguana Care
http://petiguanacare.org/taming/

Taxonomic Background – Green Iguana Society
http://www.greenigsociety.org/inthewild.htm

The Basic Types of Iguana – LizardTypes.com
http://www.lizardtypes.com/basic-types-iguanas/
What to Expect From a Pet Iguana – TheSpruce.com
https://www.thespruce.com/iguanas-as-pets-1236880

Feeding Baby
Cynthia Cherry
978-1941070000

Axolotl
Lolly Brown
978-0989658430

Dysautonomia, POTS
Syndrome
Frederick Earlstein
978-0989658485

Degenerative Disc
Disease Explained
Frederick Earlstein
978-0989658485

Sinusitis, Hay Fever,
Allergic Rhinitis Explained
Frederick Earlstein
978-1941070024

Wicca
Riley Star
978-1941070130

Zombie Apocalypse
Rex Cutty
978-1941070154

Capybara
Lolly Brown
978-1941070062

Eels As Pets
Lolly Brown
978-1941070167

Scabies and Lice Explained
Frederick Earlstein
978-1941070017

Saltwater Fish As Pets
Lolly Brown
978-0989658461

Torticollis Explained
Frederick Earlstein
978-1941070055

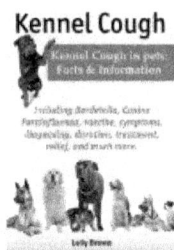

Kennel Cough
Lolly Brown
978-0989658409

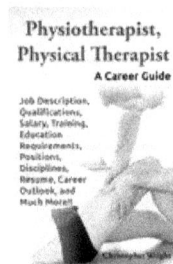

Physiotherapist, Physical
Therapist
Christopher Wright
978-0989658492

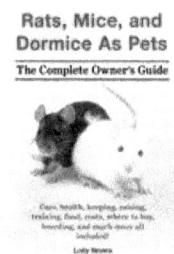

Rats, Mice, and Dormice
As Pets
Lolly Brown
978-1941070079

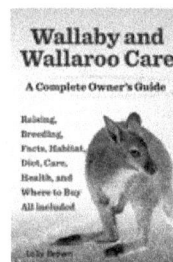

Wallaby and Wallaroo Care
Lolly Brown
978-1941070031

Bodybuilding Supplements
Explained
Jon Shelton
978-1941070239

Demonology
Riley Star
978-19401070314

Pigeon Racing
Lolly Brown
978-1941070307

Dwarf Hamster
Lolly Brown
978-1941070390

Cryptozoology
Rex Cutty
978-1941070406

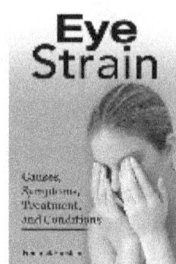

Eye Strain
Frederick Earlstein
978-1941070369

Inez The Miniature Elephant
Asher Ray
978-1941070353

Vampire Apocalypse
Rex Cutty
978-1941070321

www.ingramcontent.com/pod-product-compliance
Lightning Source LLC
Chambersburg PA
CBHW070014110426
42741CB00034B/1732